STEP-BY-STEP
Origami
& PAPERCRAFT

CHARTWELL
BOOKS, INC.

Paul
Jackson

A QUINTET BOOK

ISBN: 0–7858–0545–1

This book was designed and produced by
Quintet Publishing Limited

Art Director: Peter Bridgewater
Designer: Linda Henley
Editors: Sandy Shepherd, Judith Simons
Photographer: Andrew Sydenham
Stylists: Paul Jackson, Vivien Frank
Illustrator: Lorraine Harrison
Jacket Design: Nik Morley

Typeset in Great Britain by
Central Southern Typesetters, Eastbourne

Produced in Australia by Griffin Colour

Published by Chartwell Books
A Division of Book Sales, Inc.
P.O. Box 7100
Edison, New Jersey 08818-7100

CONTENTS

INTRODUCTION

What is classic origami? There are of course, many different opinions, but most paper-folders would agree that the very best origami is enjoyable to fold and attractive to look at. The folding sequence should be economical and flow elegantly from one step to the next, so that the design emerges seemingly effortlessly from the paper and concludes boldly, even dramatically, without any messy rounding off or tucking in. The completed design should not be scarred with unwanted creases, be misshapen or have an unnecessarily complex surface.

Perhaps most importantly though, the design should somehow be original. The restrictive 'rules' of origami (the paper may only be folded, never cut or glued) mean that *true* originality is rare and most designs, though clever, are often little more than variations on well-worn themes. A classic design must be a one-off.

If you are new to origami, please read the next few pages before starting to fold. They will make the book easy and a pleasure to use. Experienced readers may wish to skip them, but do be careful to fold within your capability: too much ambition can end in frustration, though it is sometimes fun to try something difficult. Please remember that whether you are a master or a novice, your level of ability is unimportant, so long as you enjoy what you can make. In fact, the very greatest designs are the simplest ones, so beginners take note! It isn't what you put in that can make a design a classic, but what you leave out. In origami, less is sometimes more.

I have had the greatest pleasure assembling this collection of personal favourites and hope that they will delight and inspire you.

PAUL JACKSON

PAPER

There are two types of paper for origami: ordinary paper to practise with and special paper to display your favourite designs. A particularly good practice paper is photocopying paper, which can be bought from stationers or from the photocopying print shops found in most shopping centres. Buy the paper in bulk and the cost per sheet becomes minimal. For a small sum, a print shop will trim the oblong sheets to perfect squares, saving you much labour and guaranteeing accuracy. Other excellent practice papers include writing paper, typing paper, computer paper, brown wrapping paper and even pages cut from a magazine if no other paper is available. Avoid folding newspaper, paper tissues and duplicating paper.

A favourite design folded for display will have a greater presence if made from an unusual but appropriate paper. Art and craft shops sell a wide variety of interesting papers suitable for folding, including Ingres (Strathmore) paper, pastel paper, watercolour paper and textured or marbled papers. Some large cities have shops which specialize in selling nothing but paper and these are certainly worth a visit. Oriental import shops and craft shops sell packets of traditional square origami paper, white on one side and coloured on the other. Origami paper is convenient to use and pretty to look at, but it can make some designs look gaudy. For displays, use it with care.

Consider too using unlikely papers: try folding wallpaper, old posters, paper-backed metallic foil, decorative gift-wrap paper, handmade paper or even thin card, cellophane and paper bath mats. Anything goes! Start a collection of unusual papers and experiment.

SYMBOLS

Symbols are the core of any book about origami. They need not all be learnt at once, but it is important to know at least the symbols for valley and mountain folds. When you see an unfamiliar symbol, refer back to this page to see what it means.

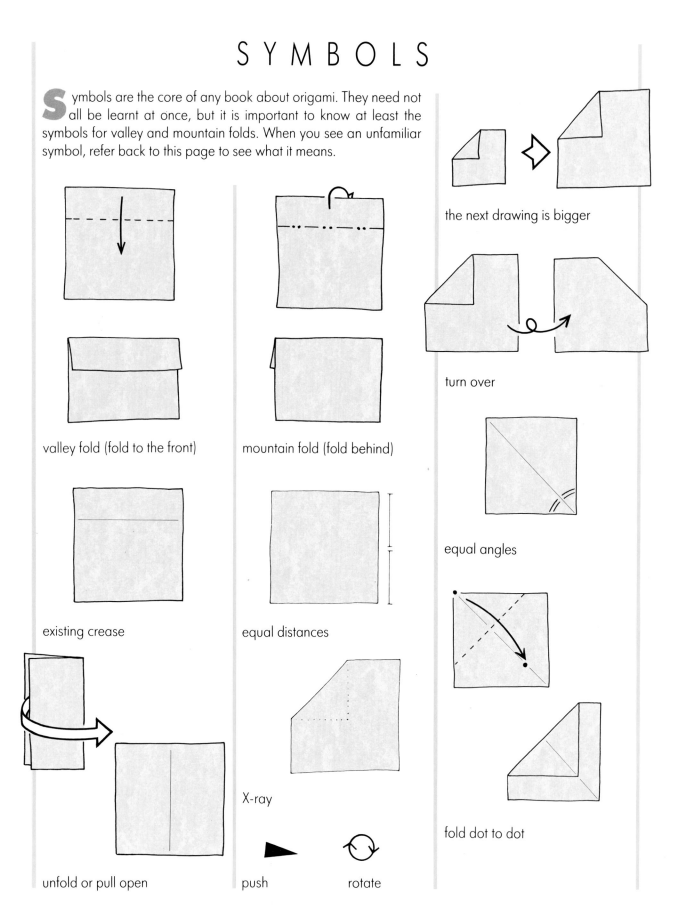

the next drawing is bigger

turn over

valley fold (fold to the front)

mountain fold (fold behind)

existing crease

equal distances

equal angles

X-ray

fold dot to dot

unfold or pull open

push   rotate

FIRST PRINCIPLES

HOW TO MAKE A SQUARE

Most bought papers are oblong and have to be trimmed square. There are several ways to do this, but here is the best.

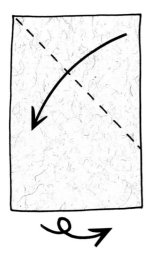

1 Fold a triangle. Turn over.

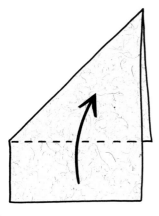

2 Fold up the oblong exactly level with the edge of the triangle behind.

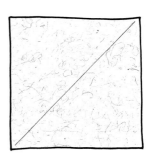

3 Cut off the excess oblong of paper with a non-serrated kitchen knife which has a blade at least 5in (12cm) long.

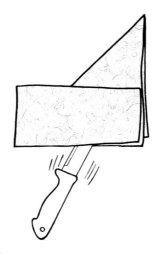

4 Hold the paper firmly against a hard, level surface and cut along the crease with a series of smooth slicing movements.

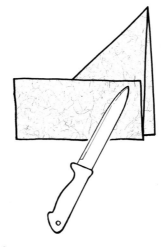

5 The completed square. Done properly, the edge is pleasingly clean.

HOW TO MAKE A CREASE

This may seem pedantic to the eager beginner, but it is important to know how to make an accurate crease. Just one inaccuracy early in a sequence will throw all the later creases out of alignment, creating a clumsy design.

The basic rule is very simple. Keep rotating the paper (or turning it over), so that every crease is made from left to right across your body (or right to left, if preferred), and the part of the paper which folds over when the crease is made moves *away* from your body, not towards it or to one side.

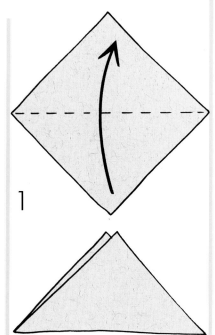

1

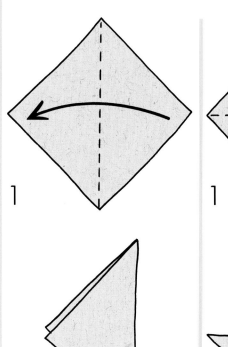

1

2 A correct crease.

When you see a crease on a diagram which does not run from left to right, *rotate the paper* so that it does, then make the crease.

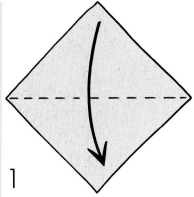

1

2 An incorrect crease.

When you see a mountain fold symbol, turn the paper over (or open up the inside), making a *valley* fold, then turn back over (or close up) again.

2 An incorrect crease.

Creases are not chores to be done as quickly as possible on the way to completing a design. They should be enjoyed. Some experts believe that the pleasure of origami lies more in the making of creases and the manipulation of paper, than in achieving a completed design, or looking at one. Take time out to *enjoy* your folding.

BASIC TECHNIQUES

REVERSE FOLD
Basic Example

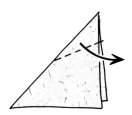

1 Fold in half.

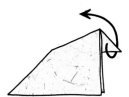

2 Fold the corner across to the right . . .

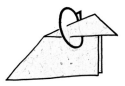

3 . . . then fold it around the back along the same crease.

4 Unfold.

5 Hold as shown. Swing the top corner down between the layers . . .

The root of paper folding is the *valley fold* (and its opposite the *mountain fold*). Such basic creases need no explanation, but more complex techniques do. The most common technique is the *reverse fold* and its opposite the *outside reverse fold* (most things in origami it seems, have an opposite). They are explained below, as is another technique, the *squash fold*. Other techniques are explained with the designs.

If you are unfamiliar with the reverse and squash folds, please take a little time to fold the basic examples and studies which follow.

6 . . . like this. Flatten the creases. The reverse fold complete.
The reverse fold described above is notated like this:

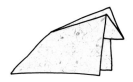

1

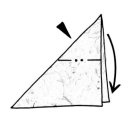

2 Reverse

Studies
Here are further examples. Look at them carefully before attempting them.

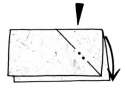

1 Reverse

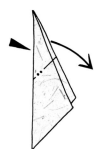

1 Reverse

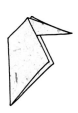

2

If you are unfamiliar with the reverse fold, prepare by folding the crease backwards and forwards as in steps 2–4 of the basic example above.

OUTSIDE REVERSE FOLD
Basic Example

1 Fold the corner across to the left . . .

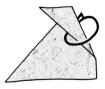

2 . . . then fold it around the back along the same crease.

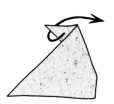

3 Unfold.

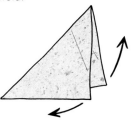

4 Spread A and B.

5 Refold both short creases as valleys, lifting C.

6 Collapse back in half.

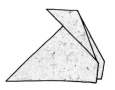

7 The outside reverse fold complete.

The outside reverse fold described above is notated like this:

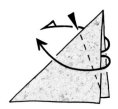

1 Outside reverse

2

SQUASH FOLD
Basic Example

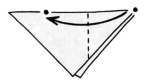

1 Fold in half.

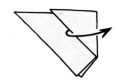

2 Fold dot to dot.

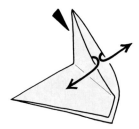

3 Unfold, so that A stands upright.

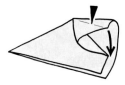

4 Squash A flat, opening the pocket . . .

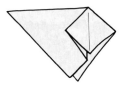

5 like this. Flatten the paper. The squash fold complete.
The squash fold described above is notated like this:

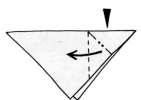

1 Squash

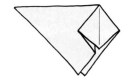

2

B A N G E R

This is one of the most entertaining of all paper folds and certainly the loudest! Practise Step 7, because good technique will increase the volume of the bang. Use a rectangle of thin or medium weight paper, at least 10×15in (25×37cm). Larger sheets will produce louder noises.

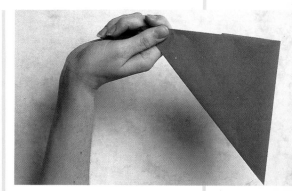

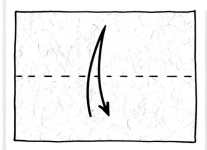

1 Fold one long edge across to the other. Crease and unfold.

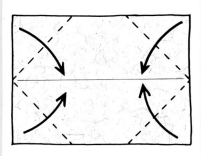

2 Fold in the corners to the centre crease.

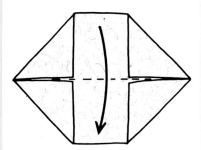

3 Fold in half along the Step 1 crease.

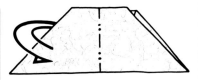

4 Mountain fold across the middle. Crease and unfold.

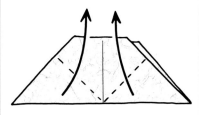

5 Check that the centre crease made in Step 1 is a mountain (if it's a valley, turn the paper over), then fold the sharp corners across to the right.

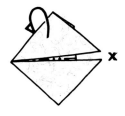

6 Mountain fold in half. Note the double corner at X.

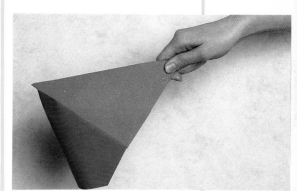

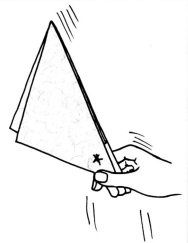

7 Hold X as shown. Bend your elbow so that the Banger is behind your head, then whip it downwards very quickly. The paper will unfold with a loud **BANG**! If it doesn't, check that you haven't held the paper upside down and try to move your arm quicker.

B I R D

Whereas some origami designs can be naturalistic, other designs, such as this one, are really symbols. Here is a bird – not a duck or a swan – just a bird: it has a head, wings and and a tail, so it *must* be one, even though it doesn't look like any particular species. Is the design a remarkable distillation of form, or merely an example of inadequate technique? Surely the former.

Use a 6–8in (15–20cm) square of paper.

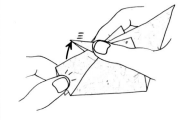

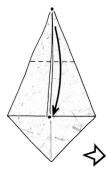

3 Fold dot to dot.

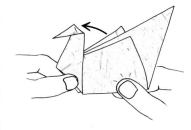

6 Lift the beak away from the neck. Squeeze flat the back of the head to make new creases.

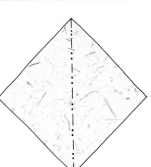

1 Make a mountain crease along a diagonal. Unfold.

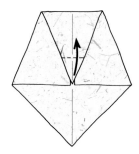

4 Fold the sharp corner back up a little way. The exact distance is unimportant.

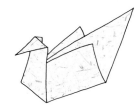

7 Lift the neck away from the body. Squeeze flat the base of the neck to make new creases.

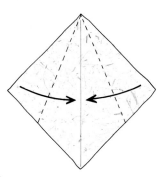

2 Fold two edges to the centre crease. Be careful to make a neat corner at the top.

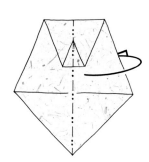

5 Mountain fold in half.

8 The Bird is complete.

C U P

Few origami designs are practical. Made from a waterproof material such as metallic kitchen foil or greaseproof paper, this simple design will hold a liquid without leaking through an open edge. Turned upside down, it will even make an excellent hat. Flap B can be brought down to form a visor. Use a 6–8in (15–20cm) square of paper.

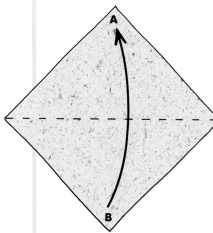

1 Fold in half along a diagonal.

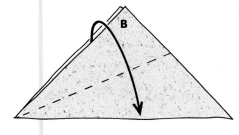

2 Fold down corner B to the bottom edge . . .

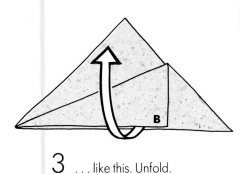

3 . . . like this. Unfold.

4 Fold one dot to the other.

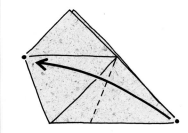

5 Fold one dot to the other.

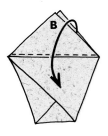

6 Fold down single layer B.

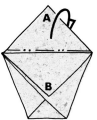

7 Fold A behind.

8 The Cup is complete.

W A T E R L I L Y

This is the full version of a spectacular napkin fold sometimes seen in restaurants. Note the remarkable manner in which the uninteresting shape made up to Step 6 is gradually opened up and transformed into the beautiful completed design. Use a paper napkin. Ordinary paper will rip at Step 7.

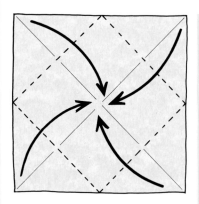

1 Fold the corners to the centre.

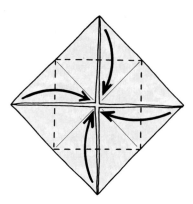

2 Again, fold the corners to the centre.

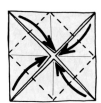

3 Once again, fold the corners to the centre.

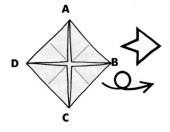

4 Turn over. Note ABCD.

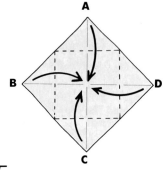

5 Yet again fold the corners to the centre.

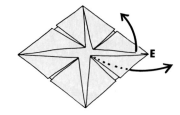

6 Note E. Hold all the layers flat and pull out corner A mentioned in Step 4.

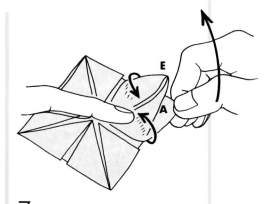

7 Hold as shown. Pull A forcibly upwards, so that it unpeels around E . . .

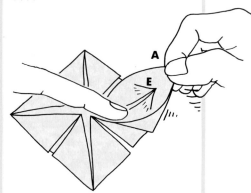

8 . . . like this. Repeat with B C and D, keeping hold of the centre.

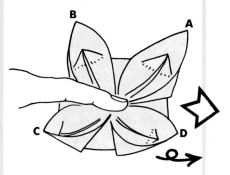

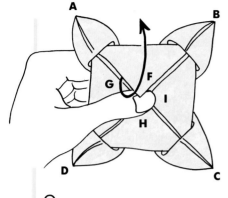

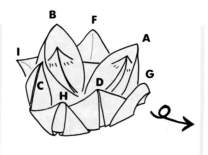

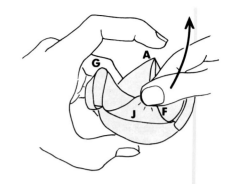

9 Turn over. Note FGHI. Lift F . . .

11 Turn over.

13 . . . and pull it up in front of A. Repeat with K L and M.

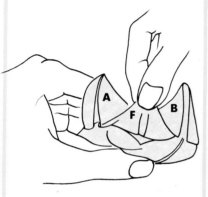

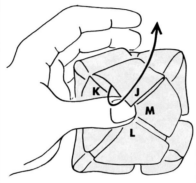

10 . . . and pull it up between A and B, as far as it will go. Repeat with G H and I, still keeping hold of the centre.

12 Note JKLM. Lift J . . .

14 The Waterlily is complete.

F L A P P I N G   B I R D

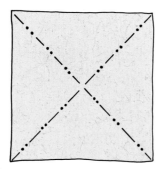

1 Mountain fold both diagonals. Unfold.

Here is perhaps the greatest of all 'action models'. The bird shape is itself satisfying, but the wide, graceful arc made by the wings when flapped is dramatic and appealing. If you want to carry an origami design in your handbag or wallet to entertain people with, this must surely be the one. Use a 6–10in (15–25cm) square of paper.

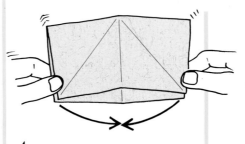

4 Hold as shown. Swing your hands together . . .

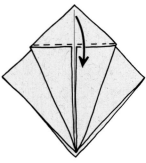

7 . . . like this. Fold down the top triangle.

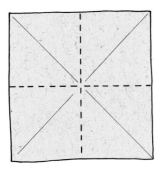

2 Valley fold horizontally and vertically. Unfold.

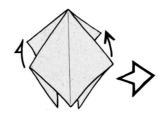

5 . . . to create this 3D star shape. If the pattern of mountains and valleys is incorrect it will not form, so check Steps 1–2.

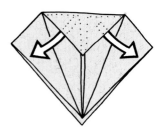

8 Pull out the side triangles.

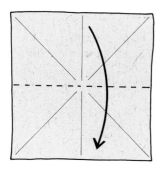

3 Fold the top edge down to the bottom along the existing crease.

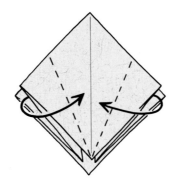

6 With the closed (neat) corner at the top, fold in the lower front edges to the centre crease . . .

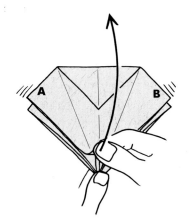

9 Take hold of just the top layer. Lift it upwards . . .

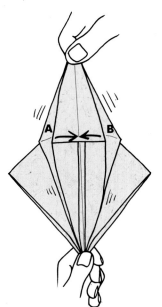

10 . . . swivelling it right up and over the top edge of the paper shape. A and B will move inwards.

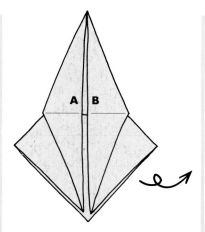

11 Flatten the diamond shape with strong creases. Turn over.

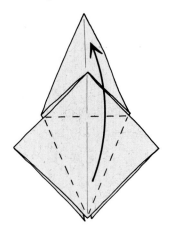

12 Repeat Steps 6–11 on this side, to make another diamond shape to match the first. Note the loose triangle hidden between them.

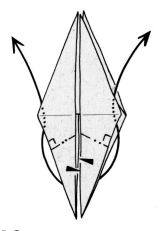

13 Reverse fold each of the lower points, so that each reverse starts a little below the centre of the diamond.

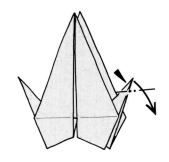

14 Reverse the head.

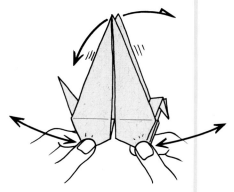

15 Hold as shown. To complete the Flapping Bird, move your hands gently apart and together, apart and together, and the wings will flap!

G L I D E R

What could be simpler – a Glider with only *two* folds! Be careful to follow the instructions carefully, because it is important to hold and release it in the correct way. There is probably an even simpler Glider with just *one* crease, waiting to be designed! Use a 6in (15cm) square of thin paper such as origami paper, airmail paper or undercopy (bank) typing paper. Heavier paper will not float the design through the air.

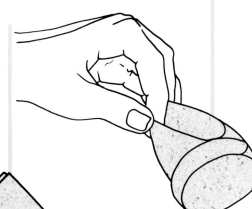

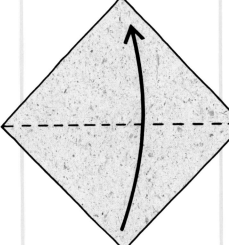

1 Fold in half along a diagonal.

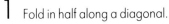

2 Fold up the lower edge a little way. Try to keep the crease exactly parallel to the edge.

3 Tuck one end of the hem into the pocket at the other end, bending the paper into a circle with the hem on the outside.

4 The Glider is complete. Make sure that the leading edge is a neat circle.

5 Hold as shown, high above your head, with the Glider pointing downwards. Release it gently. It will fall quickly at first, then level out and glide a considerable distance. Remember to release it gently. Never throw or push it.

S A M P A N

This design has a remarkable climax when, at Steps 10–12, the entire shape is turned inside-out to suddenly reveal the completed Sampan. A few other designs contain inversions to part of their structure, but none to this extent. A simpler variation is to regard Step 5 as a flat, uncreased square, then to proceed as diagrammed, but omitting Step 13 to create a boat without a canopy. Use a 6–8in (15–20cm) square of paper with different colours on the two sides. Begin by creasing both diagonals, then folding a pair of opposite corners to the middle.

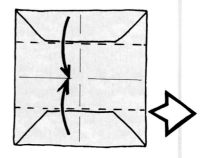

5 Fold the top and bottom edges to the centre.

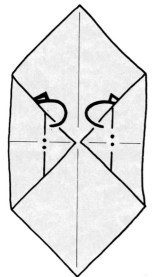

1 Tuck the corners inside.

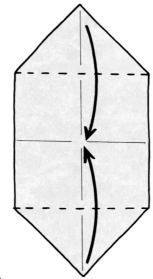

3 Fold the remaining corners to the centre.

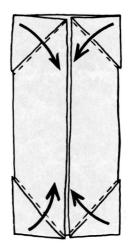

6 Turn in the triangles.

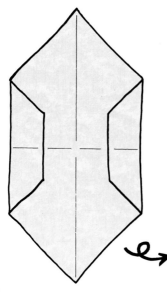

2 Turn over.

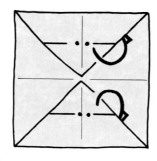

4 Similarly, tuck these corners inside.

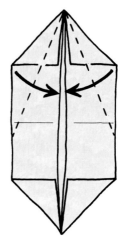

7 Narrow one end, then . . .

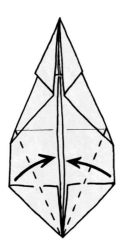

8 . . . narrow the other.

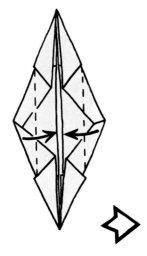

9 Fold the side corners to the centre.

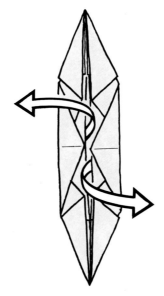

10 Pull the side layers right apart to expose a clean base . . .

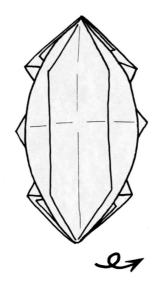

11 . . . like this. Keep the layers pressed together. Turn over.

12 The arrowed corners point towards you. Push them down with considerable force, so that they invert backwards and the Sampan turns inside-out . . .

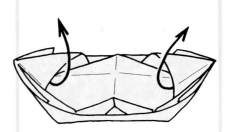

13 . . . like this. Lift up the canopies.

14 The Sampan is complete.

YOSHIZAWA'S BUTTERFLIES

Akira Yoshizawa is the single most important paper-folder in the world. He was born in 1911, at a time when origami meant little more to the Japanese than the mechanical reproduction of a few traditional designs, and when creative origami was virtually unknown. As with many children, origami became an absorbing hobby of his. Unlike other children though, it later became such an obsession that at the age of 26 he left his job in an iron foundry (where he had usefully learnt the principles of geometry) to devote himself to origami. For a decade he worked alone and in poverty, inventing many new designs and forging his philosophy of creative origami. Shortly before World War II, a twist of fate brought him much publicity and an influential patron to guide him on his professional career.

After the war, Yoshizawa resumed his career, publishing his first book in 1952, establishing the International Origami Center in 1954 and first exhibiting in Europe in 1955. Since then, he has received many cultural honours and travelled widely, including several visits to the West where origami enthusiasts have acclaimed his work.

Yoshizawa separates origami into two kinds: 'recreational' and 'art'. The former he largely dismisses as being the mechanical reproduction of a design to give an illustrative likeness of a subject, but without expression or character. Such designs include all traditional and geometric work and almost all other modern creative work, from East or West. To Yoshizawa, these designs may be clever, but they are without spirit. He advocates an origami which reveals the inner character of the subject through the interpretive skills of the paper-folder. Mere symbolic representation is not enough: the folder must have an empathy for the subject he is folding and the material he uses (the paper). If this suggests a philosophy that is too all-embracing and too emotional to be practised by the reader who wishes his origami to simply be an enjoyable pastime, then it is a measure of Yoshizawa's complete commitment to his art.

However total or controversial Yoshizawa's approach may be, there can be no doubting the quality of his work, the range and diversity of which is legendary. In particular, his finesse with paper is without equal. It is so exquisite as to defy reproduction by any other folder. Diagrams can only show the bare bones of a design, which the folder through dedicated practice must flesh out and bring to life.

The butterflies photographed here (which have all been folded by Yoshizawa and generously donated for use in the book) show a good cross-section of his work, from the very simple to the very complex, but all beautifully folded. The simpler ones can be folded by anybody, even young children. Although they are examples of the

'recreational' style which he does not usually support, they can be made to flutter when the central ridge is depressed, bringing them to life and so earning them a place in his renowned and charismatic teaching performances.

The more complex ones show his engineering prowess. Were this a Yoshizawa book, the designs would be yet more beautiful, but western writers are not usually permitted to publish the very best of his work. Indeed, visitors to his home-cum-studio in Tokyo say that the most extraordinary of his pieces remain unpublished.

It is possible to conceive that a modern origami movement would have evolved without Yoshizawa, but his genius has enriched the art for all time.

YOSHIZAWA'S
BUTTERFLY

Here are the instructions for Yoshizawa's best-known Butterfly, drawn by the creator for use in the book and reproduced without alterations or additions. This butterfly is the logo of the International Origami Center, which Yoshizawa founded to help spread friendship and peace through origami. The design is so well-known that it has almost become traditional.

Yoshizawa does not give the written step by step instructions as we have done in other designs, but by now the reader should be familiar enough with the diagrams and symbols to be able to follow his instructions.

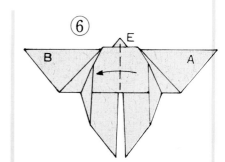

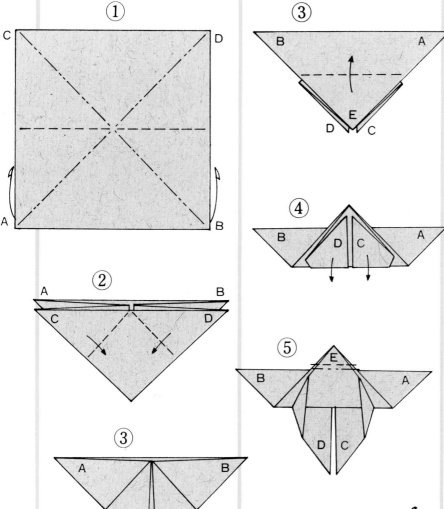

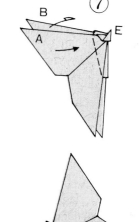

Akira Yoshizawa

23

YACHT

There are many origami yachts, boats and ships, but none are as simple or as full of movement as this wonderful design by Japan's First Lady of origami, Mrs Toshie Takahama. Mrs Takahama has produced many exquisite designs, particularly of animals and flowers. She has written several books, some of which have recently been translated into English. Use a 6–8in (15–20cm) square of origami paper.

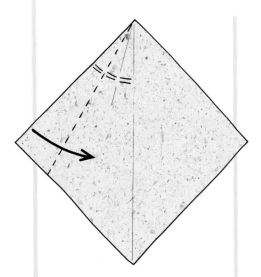

1 Fold in the top edge one third of the way towards the diagonal crease.

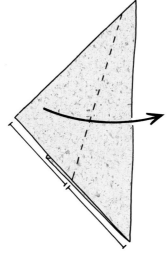

3 Fold it back along a crease which starts just to the left of the top corner and goes to the mid-point of the lower edge.

5 Mountain fold the bottom corner behind.

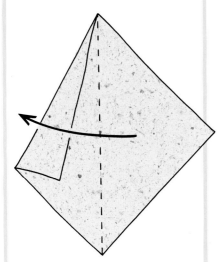

2 Fold the right hand corner across to the left.

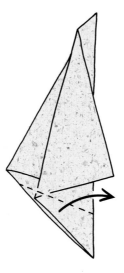

4 Fold the bottom corner across to the right.

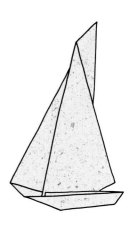

6 The Yacht complete.

CUBE

The creator of the Cube, Shuzo Fujimoto (Japan) has conducted a great deal of research into the geometry of folding, including important discoveries about how to fold accurate polygons (pentagons, hexagons, and so on) from a square; how to divide an edge into accurate thirds, fifths, etc without 'guesstimating'; and how to fold a one-piece solid such as a tetrahedron or an icosahedron. If all this sounds rather dry (it isn't!), just enjoy folding his Cube. In particular, enjoy Step 5 – surely one of the 'best moves' in all origami. Use a 6–8in (15–20cm) square of thin or medium weight paper.

1 Carefully divide the paper into quarters. horizontally and vertically, to create 16 squares.

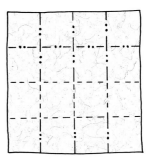

2 Re-crease the creases to look like the pattern of mountains and valleys shown here.

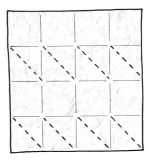

3 Add eight short diagonals. Be precise.

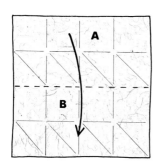

4 Fold in half. Note squares A·and B.

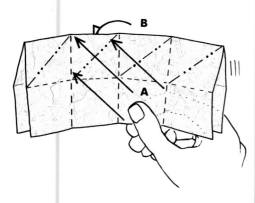

5 Hold as shown. Note square A at the front and B behind. The aim is now to slide A up and to the left so that it exactly covers B. When this has happened, the paper will have curled into a cube form. All of the marked creases *must* form cleanly and simultaneously. There is a knack to this 'slide', so please try it several times.

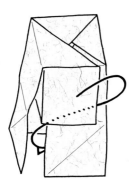

6 Tuck the front square inside to lock the top.

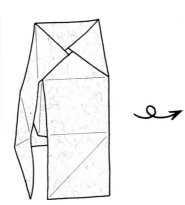

7 Turn over.

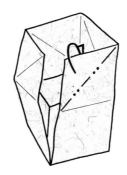

8 Fold in the corner.

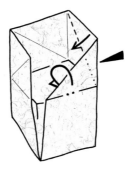

9 Push in the next corner to form part of the lid.

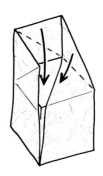

10 Push in the next corner . . .

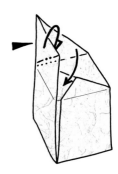

11 . . . and the next.

12 Tuck the triangle inside the cube to lock the top.

13 The Cube complete.

CAT

This is another design by Mrs Toshie Takahama. The cat is regarded by many creative tolders to be a very difficult subject to capture in paper, because its shape is very simple and curved. In the opinion of the author, Mrs Takahama's Cat is the most successful version yet achieved, being well proportioned, full of character, instantly recognizeable and pleasing to fold. The design benefits from being made from a textured paper such as Ingres (Strathmore), or another appropriate paper. Begin with Step 3 of the Bird, using a 6–8in (15–20cm) square of paper as in that design.

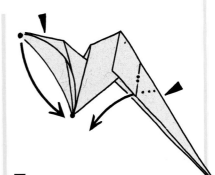

7 Squash the point, dot to dot. Reverse the tail.

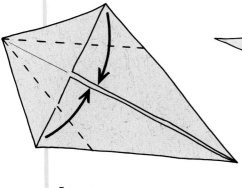

1 Fold the short edges to the centre.

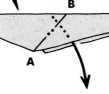

4 Reverse the blunt corner along AB, then . . .

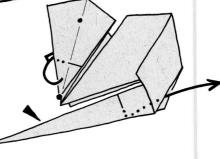

8 Tuck the point inside the face, folding dot to dot. Reverse the tail.

2 Narrow the corner at the right. Keep the corner as neat as possible.

5 . . . reverse it back up level with open edge. Reverse the sharp corner to the position shown in Step 6.

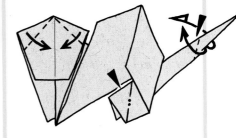

9 Fold the ears forward. Reverse the hind legs. Outside reverse the tail.

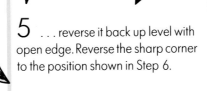

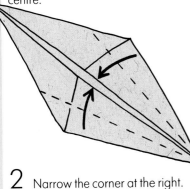

3 Fold in half. Note A and B.

6 Valley the front layer at the left across to the right, so that the point stands upright. Turn the sharp point inside out.

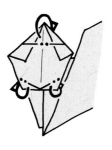

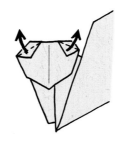

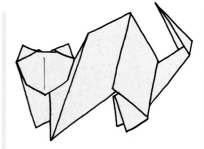

10 Shape the nose. Fold the top of the head behind.

11 Fold up the ears.

12 The Cat complete.

TULIP AND STEM

Here is the first two-piece design in the book and one of the simplest and most appealing of all origami flowers. Its creator, Kunihiko Kasahara (Japan), has written over 100 origami books – including some in English – which feature his own prolific output. To make the Tulip and Stem, make the Tulip square half the size of the Stem square, so that (for example) if the Tulip is made from a 4in (10cm) square, the Stem is made from an 8in (20cm) square. The Tulip begins with Step 6 of the Flapping Bird turned upside down and the Stem begins with Step 3 of the Bird.

BLOOM

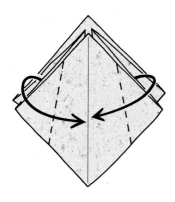

1 With the open corner at the top, fold the front corners to the centre crease. Note that the creases taper towards the top. Repeat behind.

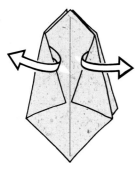

2 Unfold.

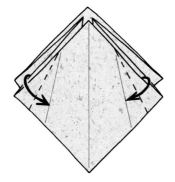

3 Fold the open edges to the crease. Repeat behind.

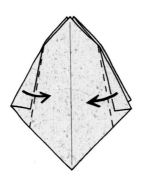

4 Fold over along Step 1 creases. Repeat behind.

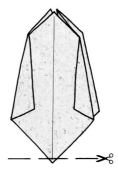

5 With a pair of scissors, snip off the tip. Snip off less than you think you should – the hole can be enlarged with another snip, but cannot be made smaller!

6 Open out.

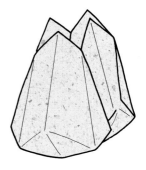

7 The Bloom complete.

STEM

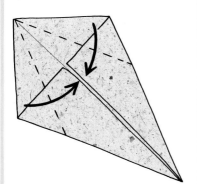

1 Fold the short edges to the centre crease.

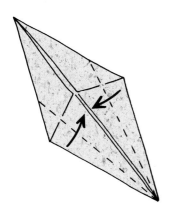

2 Narrow the bottom corner. Keep it neat.

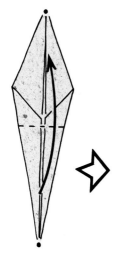

3 Fold in half, dot to dot.

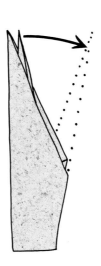

4 Pull the sharp point out to the dotted position. Squeeze the paper flat at the bottom to let the sharp point retain its new position.

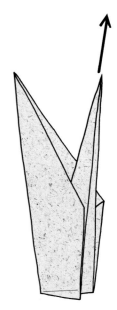

5 The Stem complete. Insert the sharp spike into the base of the Bloom.

SNAP HEXAHEDRON

Hexahedrons are common in origami. This one by Edwin Corrie (England) is one of the simplest and features an interesting move at Step 5. To make the 3 × 3 grid of squares needed in Step 1, fold a 4 × 4 grid by creasing halves and quarters horizontally and vertically, then cut off a line of squares along two adjacent edges to leave a 3 × 3 grid. Use a 6in (15cm) square of paper. Large squares will not 'snap' at Step 7.

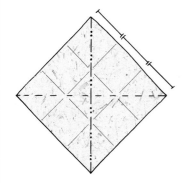

1 Fold the vertical diagonal as a mountain and the horizontal diagonal as a valley.

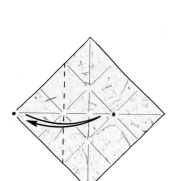

2 Fold dot to dot. Unfold.

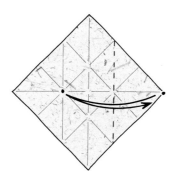

3 Similarly, fold dot to dot. Unfold.

4 Pleat as shown.

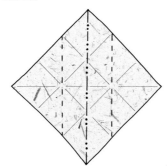

5 Outside reverse the top and bottom corners.

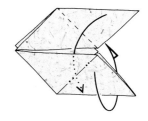

6 Valley fold the top corner into the pocket formed by the lower outside reverse fold. Then, mountain the lower corner into the upper outside reverse fold, behind.

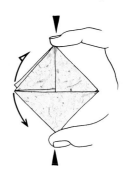

7 Hold as shown and squeeze. The left hand corners will separate to create a third edge around the middle, forming a 3D hexahedron.

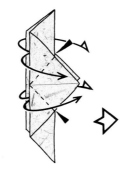

8 The Snap Hexahedron complete.

THE UN-UNFOLDABLE BOX

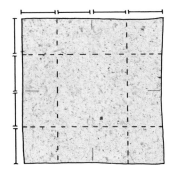

Boxes are the most common subject in origami. Some are very complex and ornate, whereas this one by Ed Sullivan (USA) is particularly plain. However, the fascination of this design *is in the folding*, because once folded, it cannot then be unfolded, at least not without making extra folds or fumbling with the paper. It is unique in origami and a remarkable design. Use a large square of medium weight paper.

1 Pinch the mid-points of the four edges. Use them as a guide to make four valley creases along the horizontal and vertical quarter marks.

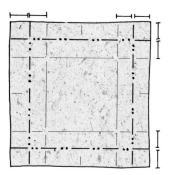

2 Make mountain folds midway between the valley quarters and the edges.

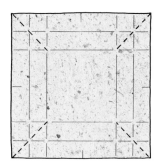

3 Form valley diagonals at the corners, to create a box with triangular flaps.

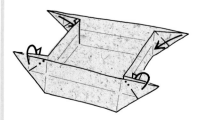

4 Point two flaps to the left and two to the right. Fold the triangles in half by turning the loose corners inside.

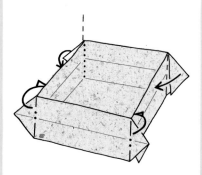

5 Fold the triangles to the inside, flat against the box.

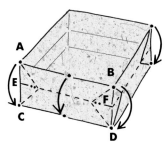

6 Collapse, bringing A down to C and B down to D. E and F move towards the centre of the front edge. Repeat behind.

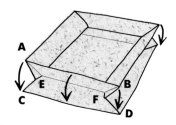

7 This is the shape half collapsed

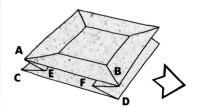

8 . . . and here fully collapsed. Note E and F.

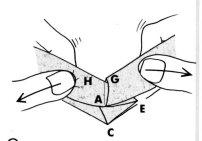

9 Hold corner AC as shown. Pull your hands gently apart and H will slide away from G . . .

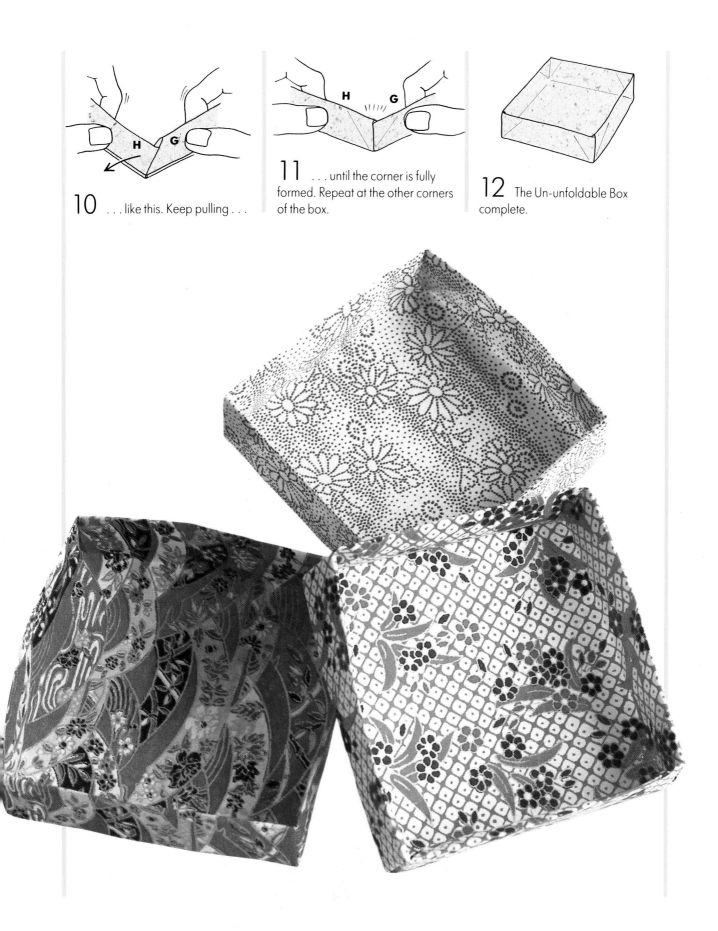

10 . . . like this. Keep pulling . . .

11 . . . until the corner is fully formed. Repeat at the other corners of the box.

12 The Un-unfoldable Box complete.

F A C E

Many liberties can be taken with the shape of a face before it becomes unrecognizable, which is why origami faces are a particularly interesting subject for creative paper folders. Not all the facial features need be present. This face by Steven Casey (Australia) – for example – does not have a mouth. Other designs may only have a nose, or just the hair, or may be extraordinarily detailed, even sculpted-looking. The shapes for this face are strong and harmonious, and the sequence is clean and flowing. Use a 6–8in (15–20cm) square of paper with different colours on the two sides.

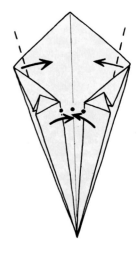

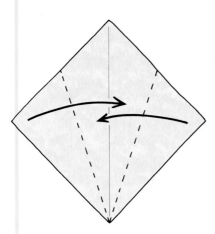

1 Fold the top corner to the left and right corners in turn, pinching the mid-points of the top edges.

3 Make creases to bisect each of the three angles on the triangular flap, so that the flap collapses to look like Step 4. Repeat on the right.

5 Swivel the triangles inwards so that they meet at the centre.

6 Fold over.

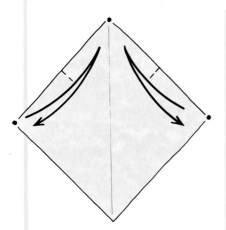

2 Make creases which connect each mid-point with the bottom corner, folding the left and right corners across the middle.

4 Turn the loose flaps inside-out, so that they change colour.

7 Repeat on the left.

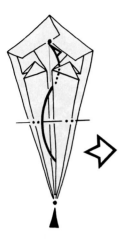

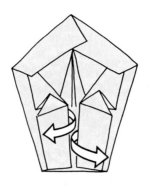

8 Reverse (or sink) the bottom point up inside the face, turning the point inside out.

9 Pull the cheeks apart to expose the point just reversed.

10 Form three creases as shown to make the point stand upright . . .

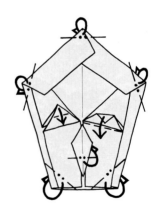

11 . . . like this. Squash it flat.

12 On the left, fold down the loose point of the eye to look like the eye drawn on the other side of the face, then fold it downwards. Blunt the nose. Round off the chin and hair.

13 The Face complete.

S T A R

rigami, like all arts and crafts, is prone to trends. The latest is 'modular' folding, in which identical units are folded and interlocked to form flat patterns, solids or stars. Some of these systems are very beautiful, perhaps profound. This Star by Nick Robinson (England) is very simple and particularly elegant in its construction. It need not have 5 points – any number greater than 2 will interlock. For a Star, use at least five sheets of square paper, either all the same colour or all different, depending on your taste. A 3in (7.5cm) square is a good size.

MODULE

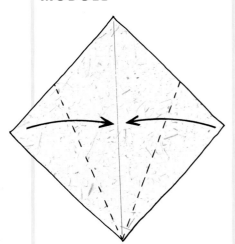

1 Fold the lower edges to the centre crease.

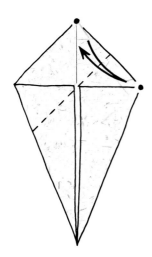

2 Fold dot to dot, as shown.

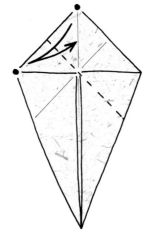

3 Repeat, but now with the opposite edge.

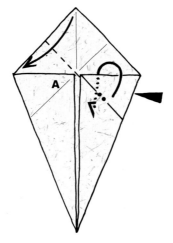

4 Re-fold Step 3, but this time reverse folding the lower right portion of the crease. Note A.

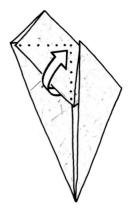

5 Pull out A to the front.

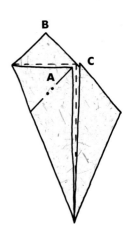

6 Crease two valleys and a mountain as shown, to give the module some shape . . .

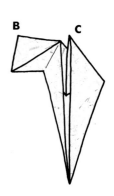

7 . . . like this. The module is complete. For a Star, make four more.

ASSEMBLY

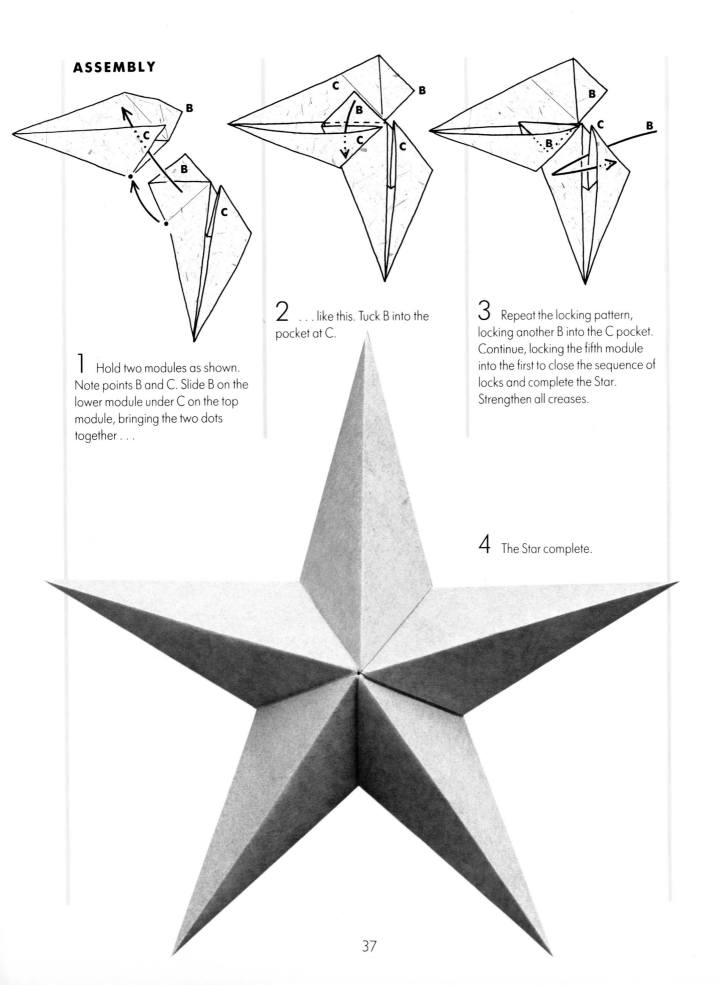

1 Hold two modules as shown. Note points B and C. Slide B on the lower module under C on the top module, bringing the two dots together . . .

2 . . . like this. Tuck B into the pocket at C.

3 Repeat the locking pattern, locking another B into the C pocket. Continue, locking the fifth module into the first to close the sequence of locks and complete the Star. Strengthen all creases.

4 The Star complete.

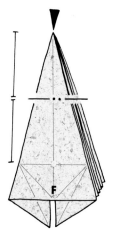

11 Invert or sink the top corner down into the body of the paper, at the level shown. Open out the hexagon to do so, then collapse it back into shape when the rim of the sink has been creased into a continuous mountain crease and the centre inverted. This is a difficult and lengthy procedure, even for experts, so persevere.

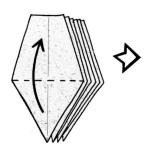

14 . . . a clean face. Fold up the bottom triangle. Repeat five more times around the layers.

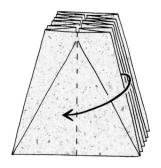

15 Fold one layer across . . .

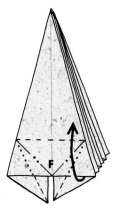

9 Lift point F along the marked creases (petal fold).

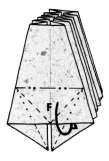

12 Tuck F up inside the front layer, reversing some of the Step 9 creases. Repeat five more times around the layers.

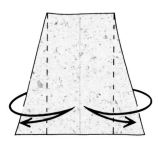

16 . . . to reveal a clean face. Note that for clarity, only the front layer will now be drawn. Crease and unfold as shown.

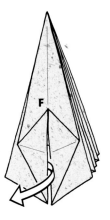

10 Unfold the Step 9 creases. Repeat five more times.

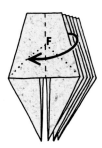

13 Fold one layer across to the left, to reveal . . .

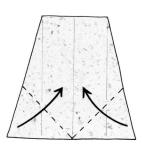

17 Fold the corners up to the centre crease.

DAFFODIL

Technically, this design by Ted Norminton (England) is the most advanced in the book and should only be attempted by experienced folders. Compare it with the much simpler Tulip and Stem the two extremes of style show how beauty can be achieved by very different means. Note the intriguing method in Steps 1–6 for folding an accurate hexagon. Persevere with the difficult 'sink' at Step 11 – practice will make it much easier. Use a medium weight yellow square for the bloom and a green square of the same size for the stem. A 10in (25cm) square will create a life-size bloom.

BLOOM

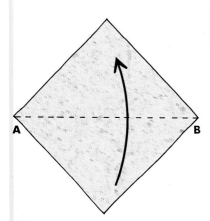

1 Fold in half along a diagonal.

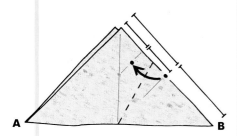

2 Pinch the mid-point and the upper quarter point. Fold the midpoint edge on to the quarter point crease, so that the new crease runs exactly to the centre of the bottom edge. Be very accurate!

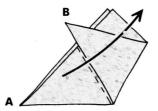

3 Fold the left corner across.

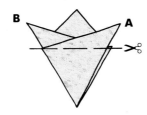

4 Cut off the upper portion of paper as shown.

5 Open out . . .

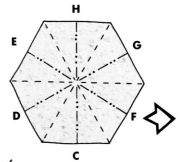

6 . . . to reveal a perfect hexagon! Crease mountains and valleys as shown, collapsing them to make Step 7.

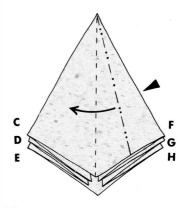

7 If the bottom edge runs straight across, turn the whole shape inside-out to make the shape seen here. Lift F and squash . . .

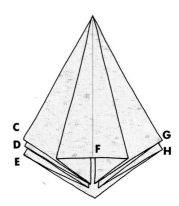

8 . . . like this. Repeat with C D E G and H. When squashing, try to keep the same number of layers left and right.

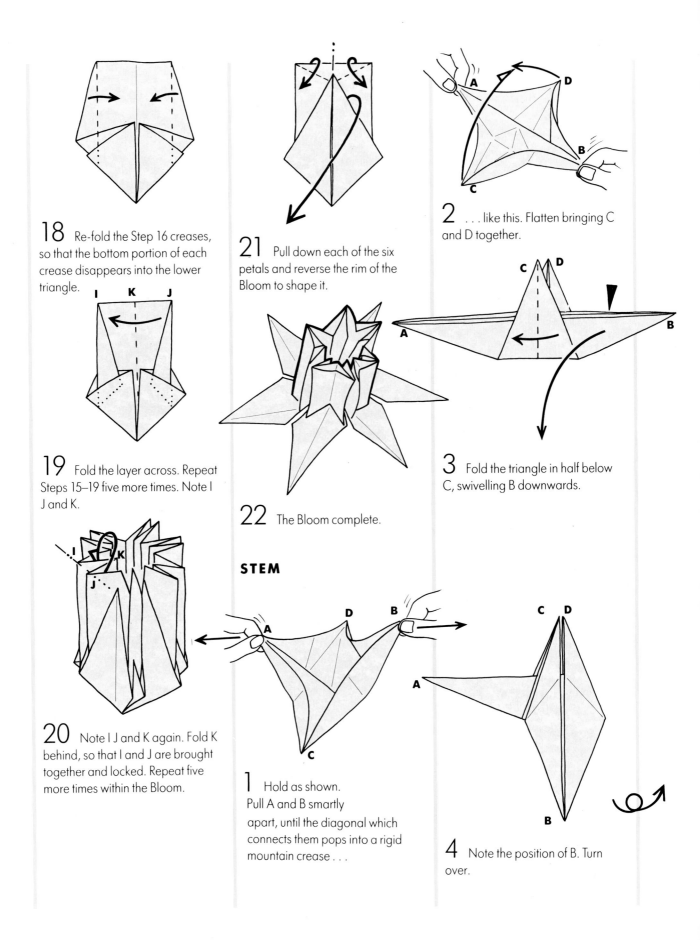

18 Re-fold the Step 16 creases, so that the bottom portion of each crease disappears into the lower triangle.

19 Fold the layer across. Repeat Steps 15–19 five more times. Note I J and K.

20 Note I J and K again. Fold K behind, so that I and J are brought together and locked. Repeat five more times within the Bloom.

21 Pull down each of the six petals and reverse the rim of the Bloom to shape it.

22 The Bloom complete.

STEM

1 Hold as shown. Pull A and B smartly apart, until the diagonal which connects them pops into a rigid mountain crease . . .

2 . . . like this. Flatten bringing C and D together.

3 Fold the triangle in half below C, swivelling B downwards.

4 Note the position of B. Turn over.

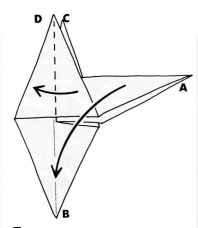

5 Repeat Step 3, swivelling A down to B.

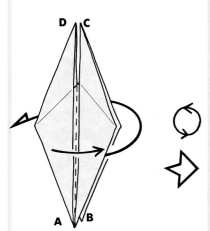

6 Fold a layer across at the front. Repeat behind but on the opposite side. Rotate the paper upside-down.

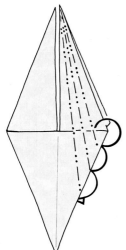

7 Narrow the front layer at the right. Repeat behind.

8 Push in or sink the bottom corner. Note that the crease tilts upward at the left. Repeat behind.

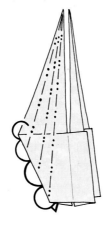

9 Narrow the flap on the left. Repeat behind.

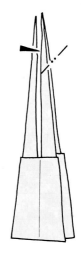

10 Reverse.

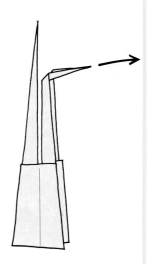

11 The Stem complete. Insert the spike into the back of the Bloom.

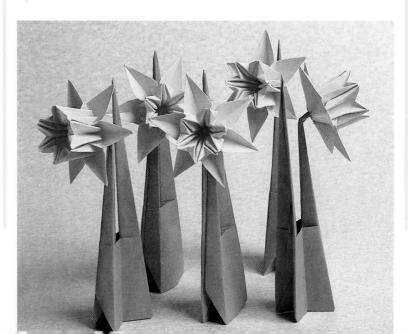

ARCHITECTURAL MODULE

This is not strictly a 'modular' design like the Star, because here there could be several different modules that lock together. The system is very much like a set of children's building blocks, which can be put together in many ways. Make as many as you can, then experiment with them to see what you can make – the photo shows just a few of the possibilities. The system is by Didier Boursin (France). Use squares of medium weight paper. 4in (10cm) squares will work well.

BAR MODULE: END LOCK

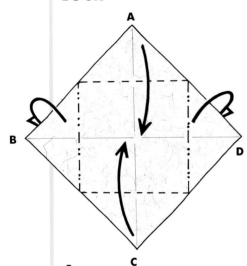

1   Valley corners A and C to the centre. Mountain corners B and D behind to the centre.

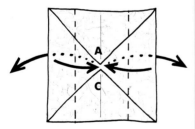

2   Fold the edges to the centre crease, allowing corners B and D to flip to the front.

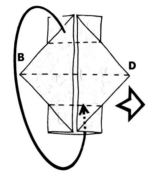

3   Crease three valleys as shown. Tuck the top edge deep inside the pocket at the bottom, locking the module into a triangular shape.

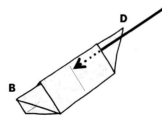

4   The completed module. The protruding triangles can lock into other modules . . .

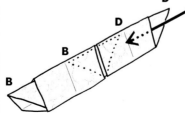

5   . . . like this. The chain can be extended infinitely.

BAR MODULE: SIDE LOCK

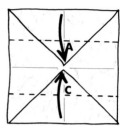

1   Begin with Step 2 above. Fold the top and bottom edges to the centre crease.

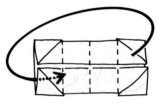

2   Crease three valleys. Tuck the right hand edge deep inside the pocket at the left edge, locking the module into a triangular shape. Allow corners B and D to flip out.

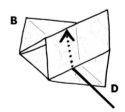

3   The completed module. The protruding triangles can tuck into other modules . . .

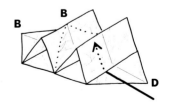

4   . . . like this. The chain can be extended infinitely.

ROSETTE

Another design by the author. The idea is a development from a known fan lock, but here done twice between Steps 7–10, once either side of the centre. The result is Step 11, which was then found to 'snap' open obligingly to hold a satisfying circular shape under tension. For storage it can be collapsed flat back to Step 10! Use an oblong of medium weight paper, twice as long as it is wide – for instance 4 × 8in (10 × 20cm).

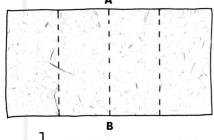

1 Valley fold into quarters. Note A and B.

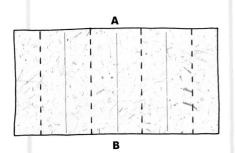

2 Valley fold into eighths.

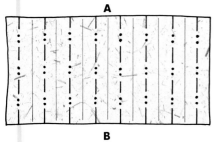

3 Place mountains between the valleys, so that . . .

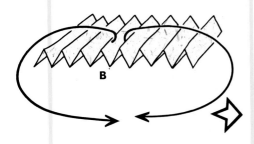

4 . . . the folds concertina together. Unfold the central crease AB.

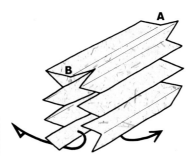

5 Unfold the first crease at each end of the pleats . . .

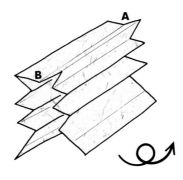

6 . . . like this. Squash the pleats flat. Turn over.

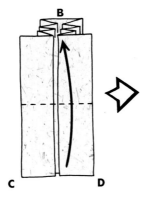

7 Fold in half. Note CD.

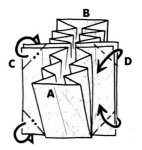

8 Allow the pleats to cascade open between A and B, but hold the central layers flat at C and D. At the right, turn in the corners with valley folds. At the left, do the same, but with mountain folds.

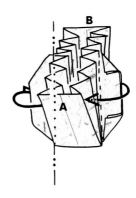

9 At the right, valley the projecting pleat into the line of pleats. At the left, do the same, but with a mountain fold.

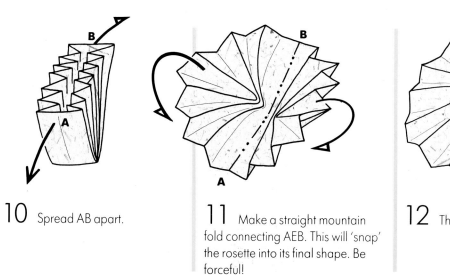

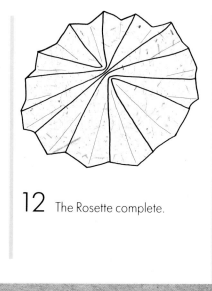

10 Spread AB apart.

11 Make a straight mountain fold connecting AEB. This will 'snap' the rosette into its final shape. Be forceful!

12 The Rosette complete.

R H I N O

The very best origami is a marriage of technology and artistry. It must be pleasing to fold and technically adept, yet still capture something of the character of the subject. The Rhino by Dave Brill (England) is a magnificent example of this school of folding. Although the steps may be followed in a mechanical way up to Step 13, the folder must then use his judgement to complete the head, tail and legs in an effective manner. Much will depend upon the choice of paper, its size and the commitment of the folder. A knowledge of the anatomy of a rhino would be of help if the completed sculpture is to be convincing. The paper will be a personal choice, but the creator recommends brown wrapping paper. Begin at Step 3 of the Bird. Use a large sheet of paper, at least 1ft (30cm) square.

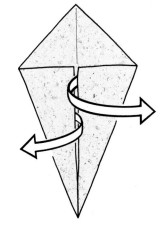

1 Unfold.

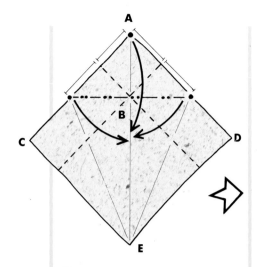

2 Crease and unfold two valleys and a mountain as shown, then collapse them simultaneously, bringing the dots together.

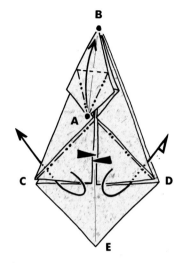

4 Lift and narrow A to touch B. Reverse the central triangles.

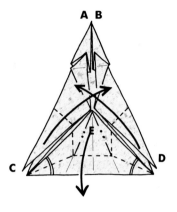

6 Fold C and D across the centre. Form five valleys and two mountains below E as shown, then collapse them to look like Step 7.

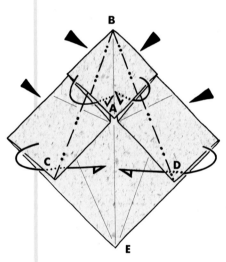

3 Reverse twice on the small top square. Reverse twice on the large side flaps, noting that the creases go exactly to corners C and D.

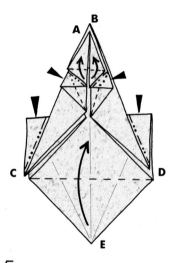

5 Form two loose triangular flaps below AB by lifting and narrowing the horizontal edges meeting at the centre. Reverse the protruding edges above C and D. Fold up E.

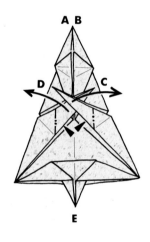

7 Reverse C and D.

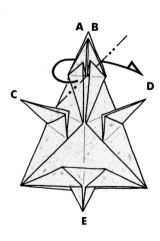

8 Swivel A and B around to the back and to the right.

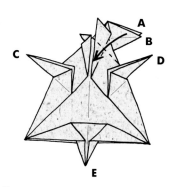

9 Valley A and B back to the front

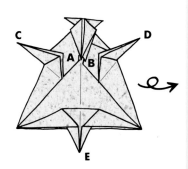

10 . . . like this! Turn over.

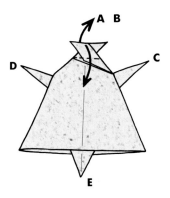

11 Fold across where shown to swivel A and B into view.

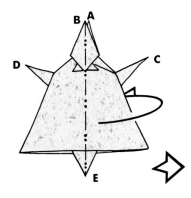

12 Mountain fold in half.

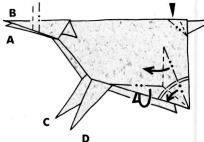

13 Pleat flap B. Reverse twice at the base of the tail. Form creases where shown on the hind leg. Repeat behind. The paper now becomes 3D.

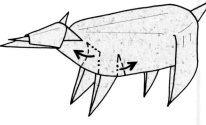

14 Shape the shoulder. Crimp the body to the rear of the foreleg. Repeat behind.

HEAD

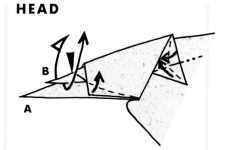

15 Outside reverse B. Lift the edge to form an eye. Collapse the ear. Repeat behind.

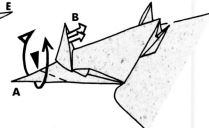

16 Pull out the inner layers at B. Outside reverse A.

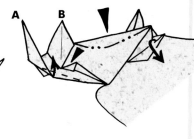

17 Lift the bottom edge to form a jaw. Squash the eye to open it. Repeat behind. Flatten the forehead.

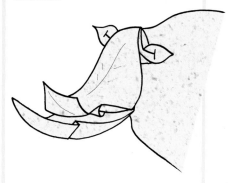

18 The head complete.

FORE LEGS

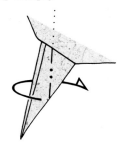

19 Mountain the leg behind, as shown.

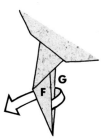

20 Separate G from F.

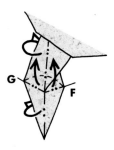

21 Collapse as shown, forming a horizontal foot . . .

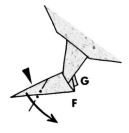

22 . . . like this. Reverse the tip.

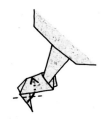

23 Tuck the point inside to lock the front of the foot shut.

24 The foreleg complete. Repeat Steps 19–24 with the other foreleg.

HIND LEGS

25 Outside reverse as shown.

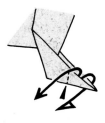

26 Outside reverse again.

27 Inside reverse the tip.

28 The hind leg complete. Repeat behind.

TAIL

29 Reverse.

30 Narrow.

31 Tail complete.

32 The Rhino complete. Well done!